Dennis Hughes, assistant pierma~~s~~ his house on The Quay, lit a cigar~~e~~ check everything was in order.

It was 1961 and Dennis had been helping his father with the arrivals and departures on the pier for some years.

This day had been no exception - there had been much to do with the arrival and departure of the *St Tudno* steamer but all was now quiet – or was it?

The Quay, Menai Bridge (Menai Heritage)

Dennis, and his father John, on duty with the arrival of St Tudno. (Vivienne Burke)

Dennis was quite used to the antics of the local children and tonight was no exception! As he approached St George's Pier he sensed movement below the deck ....

'Is that you Bowen .... how many times do I have to tell you ....

It was good sport for the local youngsters to risk the anger of the piermaster. Mike Bowen remembers how they used to go down on the shore and climb across the rocks, and up over the wall on to the promenade to avoid paying the penny entrance to the pier. Squeezing through the railings was another way of getting on for free, until one day he got his head stuck between the bars and had to have the Menai Bridge Fire Service to rescue him!

After the steamships departed, the children would climb up from the shore under the deck of the pier, where they could find coins dropped by the visitors. This is what they were doing as Dennis approached.

He wasted no more words but picked up the hose pipe to wash the deck of the pier down, in turn washing the children out, resulting in shrieks and a hurried departure!

Dennis Hughes & his father John. North Wales Chronicle, 1959 (Jennifer Jones)

With a big sigh, he turned off the water and tidied up ready for another day. No night fishermen were due so he drew on his cigarette and gazed along the Strait. Dennis was an observant and thoughtful man and he contemplated the changes due:

- his father was soon to retire, and he, Dennis, would then become Piermaster, with all the responsibilities for the management of the Quay and St George's (and later for the moorings along the Strait as well)

- how long would the passengers continue their day trips to Menai Bridge?

- the Liverpool and North Wales Steamship Company was not doing so well – there had been a fall in trade over the 1950s, changes would surely follow.

St George's Pier needed repairs and that would mean using the Quay for servicing the incoming vessels. There was plenty to do. Dennis and his father were always busy with repairs.

Dennis Hughes (Vivienne Burke)

Prince's Pier, as The Quay was now known, had always been active with imports and exports since the 1840s. Big sailing ships made speedy voyages across the Atlantic to North America from here. His Uncle Owen, like many before him, had emigrated to Canada to begin a new life. What a journey that must have been!

He remembered tales from his family about the early days of the piers; of all the timber brought from Quebec, of massive amounts of slate shipped out for roofing, and of the people who left Anglesey behind to begin a new life in a new country.

The 10th April, 1846 was a busy and exciting day on the Quay. The '*Chieftain*', already loaded with slate from Penrhyn Port, was now boarding passengers, who were emigrating to North America.

This new sailing vessel was the latest acquisition of the Davies family. **Richard Davies** and his three sons, **John, Robert and Richard**, each had a quarter share in its purchase. Richard Davies was an entrepreneur and was always ready for the latest development.

Built in New Brunswick, 1839, and bought by the Davies family in Liverpool in 1843, this 546-ton barque was 137-foot long with a shallower draft than earlier ships and thus able to make a much faster passage across the Atlantic. In 1844, she was clad in yellow metal to protect the hull from marine growth. She had a beam of 29' and a depth hold of 22' with one deck and a poop deck.[1]

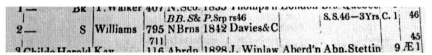

Lloyd's Register, 1847. Courtesy of Liverpool Maritime Museum Archives

[1] Aled Eames

The sheathing of the hull may have resulted in the increased tonnage given as 795 tons in 1845.[2]

The 1847 entry in Lloyds Register identifies the *Chieftain* as:

> a ship, captained by Williams, of 795 tons, built in New Brunswick, owned by Davies and Co, with an 'A' character from 1845

The seventy emigrants boarded the *Chieftain* with a mixture of excitement and trepidation. The *Immigration Papers in Canada* report that there were, on board, some respectable and wealthy emigrants from Beaumaris. These passengers were to travel on from Quebec to Illinois, to meet up with others who had already settled there.[3]

The Barque *Southern Cross*, contemporary to *The Chieftain* – lithograph by Thomas Goldworth Dutton (Robert Cadwalader)

The passengers, it seems, were pleased to be on board '*this fine vessel*'. It was owned by a respectable Methodist family with a trusted Welsh Master and an all Welsh crew.

Emigration was becoming very popular and the local newspapers were ready with advice. The *North Wales Chronicle* in 1849, gives practical advice.

> .... Look to your clothes and provide yourself with pieces for the repairs of your different garments, and an abundance of needles, thread, buttons of various sorts, hooks, eyes and strong tape ......get some common canvas tarred and dried and secured with broad-headed nails over your boxes to make them waterproof .....
>
> On the day of embarkation everything will appear in greatest disorder and sleeping arrangements may look uninviting, even miserable. Do not be disheartened as out of this apparent confusion will rise the greatest order and regularity if you are in a well-appointed ship.

---

[2] Lloyds register
[3] Irish Emigration database; Elgin Grey papers on Emigration in 1846

Once aboard begin to fasten everything upright, let nothing be loose as all will be subject to the pitching and rolling of the ship ...

Expect to be sea-sick and wonder what induced you to leave the shore .... This will not last long and by the time you gain your sea-legs the ship will be getting into essential order ...

Obey all instructions promptly - have your food ready for the ship's cook when required, put your bedding on deck when so advised and help out with food and water distribution and general cleaning duties.

Maybe John Davies, the eldest son of Richard and responsible for the shipping arm of the Davies' business, came across from his office in Packet St (now Water St) to see the *Chieftain* being towed by steam tug, under Telford's magnificent Suspension Bridge, through the treacherous Swellies, and past the preparations for the building of Stephenson's Tubular Railway Bridge, until she was able to catch the wind in her sails and get underway.

The Davies men were, however, merchants not sailors. John Davies was probably more interested in whether the *Chieftain* was on time and whether **Henry Williams** the master, would make a fast and safe voyage across the Atlantic.

Those on shore, watching this departure and waving to the travellers, may have wondered what it would be like to sail in this graceful, tall ship and set up home in another country.

Emigration Vessel — Between Decks. Illustrated London News, 10 May 1851. (National Library of Australia)

The *Chieftain* was primarily a merchant ship, though, and the crew would be preparing the vessel for the ocean voyage with little time for farewells.

The travellers now had to settle in the 'stowage', below deck and above the slate cargo. There was light and air if the weather was good - but bad weather and rough seas meant 'battening down the hatches', leaving the passengers with little light.

Once out into the open seas, the *Chieftain* would take up the wind and make good progress under the skilful master and crew with the passengers looking forward to a steady voyage across the Atlantic.

B ack on the Quay, **Owen Jones** had more work to do. For three years, he had been Deputy Manager for the *City of Dublin Steam Packet Company*, assisting with the safe arrival and departure of the trading vessels.

Steamships provided a regular service to and from the quay. Each of them needing to be loaded and unloaded. Traders from Liverpool were advised of the company requirements in preparation for sailing the following day, arriving at Menai Bridge in the afternoon.

Owen Jones, born in 1805 in Newborough, would be responsible for the disembarkation of passengers and the safe unloading of cargo. The next morning after re-loading, the ship would sail for Liverpool, whilst another steamship journeyed to Menai Bridge.

E llis William Timothy (1800-1869) was the agent for the *City of Dublin Steam Packet Co.* and would have been responsible for company bookings, as well as the facilities on the wharf including a crane. Invoices show a charge for cranage on the Davies' Wharf from 1838.

Ellis Timothy represented the company at the Caernarfon Harbour Trust meeting in a dispute about the repair of the iron crane on the Caernarfon wharf in 1847.[4]

In 1841, he is living at St George's Cottage, near Tyddyn To, in Menai Bridge with his wife Jane (nee Lloyd) and three children and is listed as an agent.

---

[4] North Wales Chronicle 19 Oct 1847

The 1846 Tithe map shows him as occupier of the Landing Pier – the land-owner being John Price Esq (of Cadnant). This landing pier would have been the Old Packet Pier.

In 1851, he is living in Rock House and is described as a steam packet agent and grocer. John Timothy, his son, is in school at Frodsham. By 1861 Ellis Wm has handed over to his son, back in Menai Bridge and listed as a packet agent.

An image of a steamship on St George's Company headed paper (Menai Heritage)

There had been a steamship service from Liverpool to the Strait since the 1820s, when Richard Davies first saw the opportunity to import goods to sell to the increased number of people coming to the area during the construction of Thomas Telford's Suspension Bridge. After its opening in 1826, traffic could cross the Menai Strait with ease, leading to a growth in population with a continued demand for goods and services.

St George's Steam Packet Company sailed regularly from St George's Pier in Liverpool bringing both goods and passengers.

Conditions aboard were very different from the passenger deck of the *Chieftain*.

Daily Communication, between North Wales and Liverpool, by the ALBION, CAMBRIA, & DRUID, STEAM PACKETS. One of these superior and well-known Packets leave BANGOR FERRY* every morning, at eight o' clock, for LIVERPOOL, calling at Garth Point (Bangor) and Beaumaris .... Breakfasts, Dinners, and Refreshments, may be had on board, at moderate charges.

N. B. All the above vessels have separate Cabins for Ladies, and are fitted up with every convenience.

North Wales Gazette, 1 May 1823

Another notice suggests the early Packet Steamers were not able to get inshore and needed boats to assist with off-loading.

Wanted, at Bangor Ferry*, a person who has BOATS to attend on the Packets. For further particulars, enquire of William Critchlow, Beaumaris, on or before 5th April

North Wales Gazette, 23 March 1825

*the name for Menai Bridge before the Suspension Bridge

The Old Stone Pier (Menai Heritage)

Passengers were increasingly using the steamers, but access to the shore was difficult. In 1835, *St George's Steamboat Packet Company* had built a stone pier, the first to stretch out into the Strait, to make it easier for passengers to disembark and for goods to be unloaded. It was known as St George's Packet Pier.

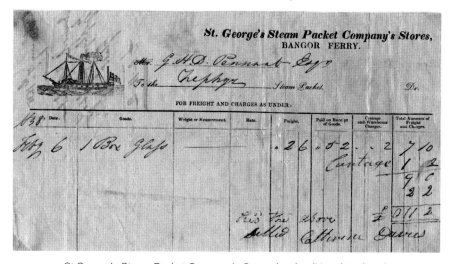

St George's Steam Packet Company's Stores invoice (Menai Heritage)

An 1838 invoice from *St George's Steam Packet Company*'s Stores at Bangor Ferry was signed by Catherine Davies, older sister of John. Cranage and warehouse charges were 2d for a box of glass for GHD Pennant Esq, of Penrhyn Castle.

In 1843, when the *City of Dublin Steam Packet Co* took over the passenger and cargo business of *St George's Steam Packet Company*, it seems they leased, from the Davies family, the part of the quay to the south of the timber quay and facing the Strait.

Founded by Charles Wye Williams in 1823 and based at Eden Quay, Dublin, the *City of Dublin Steam Packet Co* (so called because it carried the mail) first ran a service from Dublin to Liverpool.

As well as the daily work with the arrivals and departures of the steamers, Owen Jones was now expecting a new vessel, specially built for the Liverpool and Bangor (Ferry) route to join the service.

North Wales Chronicle, 28 Apr. 1846 (Menai Heritage)

The *Prince of Wales* became the most well-known steamer in the City of Dublin Company's Welsh fleet and is seen here in later years at the Quay (Prince's Pier).

Commanded by **W H Warren** RN and built on the Clyde in 1846, this '*splendid and powerful new iron steamer*' plied regularly between Menai Bridge and Liverpool.

Of 532 tons and 176.3 feet in length with a 200- horse power engine, she had a raised quarterdeck with one

Prince of Wales at Prince's Pier (Menai Heritage)

funnel abaft of the paddles and three masts, which were reduced to two in 1851.

On Mondays, Wednesdays and Fridays, she sailed from Menai Bridge at 10am and on Tuesdays, Thursdays and Saturdays she left St George's Pierhead in Liverpool at 11am.the cabin fare was 6 shillings in 1848, and the deck fare 2/6d.

In addition, she was making short break pleasure trips to and from Dublin.

The new Iron Steam Ship PRINCE OF WALES, WH Warren RN Commander is intended to leave MENAI BRIDGE for DUBLIN on SATURDAY 11th JULY at 4 o'clock in the afternoon, calling at Bangor, Beaumaris and Amlwch for passengers.... Leaving Dublin on Monday 13th July ... the cabin fare for the trip (including fees) 15s

North Wales Chronicle, 16th June 1846

All these voyages required the services of the men on the Pier to see the passengers safely aboard and to load and unload the cargoes.

J uly was also the month for the *Chieftain* to return. After a fast crossing, she had arrived in Quebec 21st May 1846.

ARRIVAL OF THE CHIEFTAIN AT QUEBEC. The *Chieftain* of Beaumaris*, **Henry Williams**, master, which sailed from the Menai on the 10th April, with 70 passengers, arrived at Quebec the 21st May, having made the passage in five weeks, taking leave of many vessels that started before her on the voyage. The letter which we have seen came by the Halifax mail, at Liverpool on Sunday last, and speaks in the highest terms of the attention of the master to the emigrants, who seem to have had a pleasant enough time of it, making light of the hardships, troubles and difficulties of a trip across the Atlantic.

Carnarvon and Denbigh Herald and North and South Independent, 20th June 1846

*Registered in Beaumaris

After only a month in Quebec, she was loaded up with a cargo of timber and ready for the return journey.

Timber yard & Prince's Pier, 1960s. (Fiona Rowlands)

The Davies' Timber Yard at Porth Daniel, was much used in the building of the Suspension Bridge (1819-1826) and was run by William Hughes of Llandrygarn but was taken over by John Davies in 1830 (aged only 21). A lease from the Marquess of Anglesey had been drawn up for the Davies family in 1828 to cover the land, including a warehouse, timber yard, sawmill and appurtenances but it was never completed.

In the 1841 census, John Davies was listed as a merchant living in the Warehouse on Packet St. *Y Cei* (the Quay) is not identified. There are however, men named with trades such as sawyer, carter and labourer living close by and most likely working at the Timber Yard.

When the Davies family bought the *Chieftain*, in 1843 they were already importing timber from Liverpool but this new vessel meant a faster voyage, straight to Quebec with slate and emigrants and a fast return with timber to the Menai Strait.

Difficulties were inevitably encountered. Timber stowage was difficult under icy conditions in North America, resulting in unstable loading. There were cholera epidemics and rough weather. Some ships were lost but the business thrived.

John Davies died in 1848 and then his father Richard in 1849, leaving Robert and Richard to run the business. There was re-organisation and the shipping section was named **R Hughes & Co**, the grocery supplies **E Edwards** and the Timber Yard became known as **William Roberts and Co**, a firm which continued landing timber on the quay by Porth Daniel until the 1970s.

James **Greaves** and his son, **Alonzo**, were contractors for the woodwork of the Britannia Tubular Railway Bridge. They needed strong scaffolding to be able to lift the masonry into position on the three great towers and to support the building of the shorter tubes over the shore in situ.

Edwin Clarke in his report written in 1846, describes the work as an '*admirable piece of construction with the regularity of bays and cross struts giving it a picturesque appearance*'

Alonzo was newly married when he came to work on the Britannia Bridge. He must have heard much about North America, when doing business at the Timber Yard. He would see the *Chief-*

Scaffolding around Caernarfon tower, Edwin Clarke, 1846 (Menai Heritage)

Alonzo Greaves in 1862 wearing his full uniform for the Union Army (the North). (Claudia Moore)

tain return from Quebec and listen to the tales of the passengers. Some six hundred people sailed from Anglesey during the 1840s.

When he finished his contract on the Britannia Bridge, Alonzo decided to take his family and emigrate to America. He sailed in 1851, but his wife, Mary, was expecting their third child and so went to relatives and followed later. In 1857, they moved on to Illinois but he was soon involved with the US Civil War.

Alonzo is seen here in his full uniform for the Union Army (the

North). He enlisted with Company A, 95ᵗʰ Regiment of the Illinois Volunteer Infantry, as a Private, serving three years (1862-1865). He later received a pension after suffering heatstroke whilst in service.

Following the Civil War, they 'homesteaded' in Iowa, settling and improving 160 acres, which, after the required 5 years, became their own.

Now the *Chieftain* was back, her shallow draft allowing her to sail up the Strait, assisted by the power of the tide – a welcome sight for those on the Quay. Too big to moor on the Quay she would drop anchor in the Strait. Boatmen would transfer passengers to the shore, where they could continue the journey by horse-drawn carriage. Soon the railway would provide yet an even easier means of travelling to Chester and on to London.

The cargo of timber from Quebec would be unloaded on to rafts and floated in to the sheltered waters near the shore and then delivered to the Timber Yard at Porth Daniel. **Thomas Roberts**, age 23, and **William Jones**, aged 42, are both listed in the 1851 census as boatmen living nearby.

This was not always an easy manoeuvre and some rafts were lost in the pull of the tide.

The *Chieftain* was re-loaded with slate from Porth Penrhyn and then 200 emigrants embarked at Menai Bridge, before sailing for Quebec.

In 1851 Richard Davies was living in Min y Don, the house built by his brother John, next to the Davies' warehouse. He is described as a shipowner and timber merchant. It seems that the Davies family kept firm control of their ships and cargoes from the office in Packet St, whilst others including Owen Jones dealt with the practicalities on the quay.

Richard Davies had always kept a trade in grocery goods (E Edwards & Co) taking deliveries for local people.

Owen Jones signed the invoice (1857), when the *Prince of Wales* brought tobacco, flour, rice, and vinegar for Lewis Parry, the shopkeeper in Pentraeth. There was a charge for wharfage and warehousing in both Liverpool and Menai Bridge.

Invoice from City of Dublin Company's Stores (Menai Heritage)

The grocery business continued to flourish for the next century and in the 1950s, Geraint Edwards' father was a sales representative for the firm. Growing up in Menai Bridge, Geraint remembers swimming in the Strait, pottering round the shore and rescuing the world from the fierce Red Indians on Bonc Fawr!

In the 1851 census Owen Jones, labourer, is living with his wife Ellen and son Owen, in the Storws (Storehouse).

The *City of Dublin Steam Packet Co* appears to be using both the stone pier, built by *St George's Steam Packet Co*, and the Davies' wharf for the mooring of their steamers.

The 1840s were busy and profitable years for the Davies family. As well as the *Chieftain*, they invested in more fast ships – all sailing out from Menai Bridge with slate and emigrants and returning with timber for use in the quarries and the building trade as well as for the Britannia Bridge.

Voyages were also made to New York and Boston. During 1847/8, 23 voyages of the Davies' ships used the Quay.[5] In addition, the steamships now ran a daily service on the North Wales route, for goods and passengers. Menai Bridge was a busy port.

Ellen and son Owen. Plot A139, St. Tysilio

Owen Jones, was living at Y Cei (Old Quay) in 1855 when his wife, Ellen, died. In 1860 his son, Owen, also died, age 22 years.

The entry for 1861 shows him as a widower, age 55 years and listed as living at *Packet Wharf*, where he is storekeeper. *Packet Wharf* refers to the steamship packet company. **Jane Evans** age 22 an unmarried servant is also at the Packet Wharf House.

At his death in 1878 Owen Jones is 73 years old and is shown as Deputy Manager for the *City of Dublin Steam Packet Co*, since 1843.

Er cof am/Owen Jones/Y Cei, Porthaethwy/Yr hwn a fu farw Gorphenaf,1878/Yn 73 mlwydd oed/Bu yn Is-Oruchwyliwr i'r City of Dublin Steam Packet Company/ Am 35 o flynyddoedd/hefyd Elizabeth Jones, ei briod/yr hon a fu farw Ionawr 1af,1890/yn 79 mlwydd oed

Owen Jones, plot B018 St. Tysilio

[5] Aled Eames

In 1904 when the new St George's Pier was opened, Mr J Davies Jones remembered how, when he was a boy, he often helped old Owen Jones, the piermaster, with the chains (a heavy safety measure replaced by handrails on the new pier).

Trade was becoming global. Ships sailing to Australia and South America needed to be bigger, with room for more cargo. Robert and Richard Davies had to make some changes. The *Chieftain* and some of the other sailing ships and barques were sold.

Larger ships needed greater docking facilities and were now sailing from Liverpool and London. By the 1860s the Quay was no longer used for long-distance shipping.

The last of the Davies' big sailing ships to leave Menai Bridge was the *Lord Stanley* in 1868. Having arrived in August with timber from Quebec, she sailed in September for Cardiff and then on to Montevideo and the Gulf of Mexico.

James Black sailed on the *John Davies* in 1852 and the *Lord Stanley* 1854 and 1855, both Davies' ships. Born in Heligoland, James came to the Menai Strait to work on the Britannia Bridge. His maritime skills would have been useful in its construction.

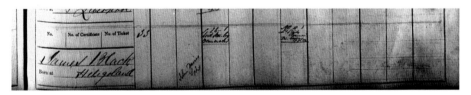

Crew List for James Black (Phyllis Barlow)

Aled Eames writes in detail about sailing on the Davies' ships in *Ventures in Sail*. The Davies brothers, Robert and Richard, and their employees, were business men, with little interest in the lives of their Masters or crew. Wives of the Masters were generally not allowed to sail with their husbands nor was time allowed for sickness.

James Black was a 'rigger', so up the ropes he would have gone, in gale force winds and icy conditions, on the voyage to Australia and South America.

With larger ships, there were larger cargoes and the Davies' ship-masters were given instructions to take care of the vessel and the cargo above all else. These were the bulk carriers of the era.

Life it seems was not too precious. This attitude was not uncommon – in the quarries on the Strait a newspaper report said that *'it was easier to replace a man than a vessel or a wheelbarrow or a boring iron ....'*[6]

The *John Davies* was an emigrant ship, travelling to Victoria, Australia, then across the Pacific to the West Coast of America to pick up a load of guano (fertiliser) for the return. This was a most unpleasant but very profitable cargo. Yellow fever was a real risk and there were many deaths including that of the captain, Richard Hughes of Beaumaris.

She left Menai Bridge carrying general goods and 450 passengers. According to diaries of the passengers, when she arrived in Portland Bay the passengers were singing psalms. Over the 110 days voyage, there had been religious services in English, Welsh and Gaelic. Praise was given for the captain and the crew, particularly those, like James Black, who worked aloft in the rigging in harsh conditions. It had not been an easy journey with sea-sickness and dysentery rife within the over-crowded vessel. There were 27 deaths on the voyage, many of whom were children.[7]

James Black & his wife (Phyllis Barlow)

James Black eventually returned to Liverpool and Menai Bridge. In later life, he retired from the sea and set up a painting and decorating business in the town.

However, whilst the bulk carriers were sailing the world, trading to Menai Bridge continued. Smaller ships maintained the regular transatlantic voyages

---

[6] The Industrial Scenery of the Kingdom II , North Wales Chronicle Tues April 4th 1848
[7] Aled Eames

with slate and emigrants to North America and timber back to the Strait. The *City of Dublin Steamers* continued to bring passengers and goods daily. All these goods and passengers had to be safely off loaded.

In 1871 Owen Jones, still living on the Quay (Packet) is listed as a Store Keeper. He has remarried. In his last years, he must have been pleased to have the enthusiastic young men such as J Davies Jones, helping with the arrival and departures of the vessels.

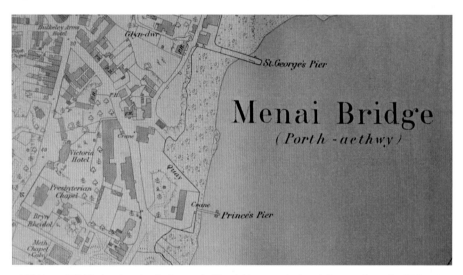

OS Map of 1889 showing the St George's Pier (old stone pier) and the new iron pier (Prince's Pier) and the crane. (Menai Heritage)

The map of the waterfront by John Haslam (around 1860) identifies the wharf in front of Bonc Daniel, with a building thereon, as **PIER** and also identifies the stone pier perpendicular to the shore at Bonc Mostyn as the **Old Packet Pier**.

There had been difficulties with the leases for this land since the Davies family first used it but, in 1866, the *Office of Woods, Forests and Land Revenues* returned a schedule of properties stating that the saw mill and smithy, the timber yard and quay, the Wharf and the warehouse facing the Strait (later known as Prince's Pier) had been occupied by the Davies family for considerable time with the Packet Pier and the storehouse offices being let to *City of Dublin Steam Packet Co.*

In January 1873, the *City of Dublin Steam Packet Co* was granted a sanction by the Board of Trade, to improve facilities for the passengers arriving at the Wharf, with acknowledgement of Crown rights over the foreshore and seabed.

The girder bridge at Prince's Pier

The outcome of this was a pier described as an iron girder bridge resting one end on the wharf and the other on a wooden pile pier, erected at the low water mark. A pontoon was fixed at the seaward end to be removed in winter when the steamers stopped their sailings.

The Liverpool landing stage, where the big Atlantic sailings began, was called Prince's Landing (or Pier). The North Wales Steamer Service also ran from here. It was logical therefore to call this new iron pier Prince's Pier – the other end of the service and landing for the *Prince of Wales* and the *Prince Arthur*.

John Hughes was only 20 years old, in 1873, when the *City of Dublin Steam Packet Co* took over the lease of the Quay and he began to work for them. John Timothy had died in 1868 and it seems John Hughes took over the role of shipping agent.

His obituary (Carnarvon & Denbigh Herald 24th July 1908) describes him as Piermaster from this date but it was not until 1902 that he was officially appointed as Piermaster & Harbourmaster and Collector of Dues by Menai Bridge Urban District Council.

John Hughes 1854 - 1908, (Vivienne Burke)

He was so well-respected that, when he died, the *Liverpool and North Wales Steam Ship Co*. steamers flew their flags at half-mast.

He and Margaret, his wife, lived in the house on the Quay and brought up their family there. It was not easy for them. They had ten children but only three sons and one daughter survived into adulthood; Owen, who emigrated to Canada, John Gray, who became the next piermaster, William Richard and Catherine Jane. Regardless of his tragedies, John continued his years on the Quay with good grace.

Margaret Hughes, John's widow, on the right, with Mary Hughes, John's sister, Ifor Williams, Mary's grandson, and his nanny, 1932. (Jennifer Jones)

The Hughes family grew at quite a pace as John's sister, Mary, married Owen Hughes, brother of Margaret, John's wife. This photo taken about 1932 shows Margaret Hughes, John's widow, aged about 84 with Mary Hughes, her sister-in-law, aged about 75, with Mary's grandson and his nanny/nursemaid. They appear to be enjoying a rest on the pier.

However, by 1878 there were complaints about the *City of Dublin Steam Packet Company*'s monopoly of the two piers in Menai Bridge. The old stone pier and the iron bridge on Prince's Pier were the only ones on the Strait.

Attempts were made by the District Council to arrange reclamation of the land along the shore. The Davies family had encroached this area and access to the Timber Yard was across it.

STEAMER ACCOMMODATION AT MENAI BRIDGE. A correspondent says: The inconvenience to which the inhabitants of Menai Bridge and its neighbourhood have long been subjected, owing to the monopoly enjoyed by the *City of Dublin Steam Packet Company* of access by water, this Company have leased the only two piers of which this portion of the Menai Straits is possessed, and exercising their special privileges for about only three months in the year, will be removed after the present season. The lease of the lower pier (old stone pier) expires this year, and, it is understood, will not be renewed, and the pier will be thrown open for the unloading of all steamers. The owner of the pier has agreed to make the necessary approaches, and the parish, recognising the value of the undertaking to the district, has agreed to give a small portion of land to render the approach on one side more accessible. As regards the other pier, which is leased to the Company by Messrs Hughes, timber merchants, it having been ascertained that the only approach forms portion of the land belonging to the parish, and which has been enclosed by Messrs Hughes, it is probable that some modification will be made in the terms of the lease, and the monopoly removed to a great extent.

North Wales Chronicle, 16th March 1878

The leases of the *City of Dublin Steam Packet Company* were terminated. This allowed for all steamers to use the landing facilities of both piers for passengers and goods. Access to the stone pier was improved. There was room for growth. Other companies could now bring goods and passengers to Menai Bridge.

The St Elvies paddle steamer at Prince's Pier between 1896 and 1903 (Menai Heritage)

The tourists continued to enjoy trips to Menai Bridge and John would be responsible for the safe arrival and departure of vessels such as the *St Elvies* (*Liverpool and North Wales Steamship Co*), seen here moored at the iron bridge pier on the Quay, sometime between 1896 and 1904.

The iron pier and the crane can be seen in front of the warehouse and the chimneys of the piermaster's house on the end of the building – the stone pier would be behind the camera and the footpath used by the visitors became the promenade.

The *Liverpool and North Wales Steam Ship Co* added to their fleet in 1899 with the Snowdon paddle steamer, seen here arriving at Prince's Pier.

Snowdon passenger paddle steamer arriving at Prince's Pier, between 1899 and 1903 (Menai Heritage)

John (Jack) Roberts was a sailor who lived in the cottages of Tan y Bont, with his wife Margaret and their children in 1871, 1881.

By 1891 he is listed as a general labourer and in 1901 as a mariner. He is said to have been assistant piermaster in the 1880s/90s.

John Hughes and Jack Roberts would have supervised the incoming and outgoing vessels from both the stone pier and the iron girder pier.

However, the old stone pier was now becoming dilapidated. There were so many visitors using the steamers

Jack Roberts. (courtesy of the Anglesey Archives - WSP/301)

and with the daily cargo unloading as well, it became preferable to use the Davies' Wharf in front of the warehouse.

In 1897 the Council decided to build a new pier and promenade for the benefit of the visitors. It was intended to develop a seaside resort in Menai Bridge and keep pace with other towns on the North Wales coast. There were difficulties though. There was a shortage of a water supply and visitors were often restricted in their use of water.

The lack of sufficient water to supply the steamers resulted in fewer vessels calling at Menai Bridge.

A bill was promoted by the Urban District Council to improve the water supply and to build a new pier. There were those in favour and those against.

Mr Walter Jones, solicitor, swore that there was a majority of 221 in favour of the pier and said that the commercial success of the place depended upon having a new pier.

Cpt Wm Smart of the *St Tudno* said that the St. George's Pier would be easier to get to if the act were passed.

Mr John James Webster, re-called, gave evidence as to the plan of the proposed new pier. He did not think the enlarged pier would obstruct the navigation of the Straits.

And showed that the new pier would not interfere with the navigation of rafts to Messrs Roberts' sawmills. To a certain extent, the extension of St. George's Pier would protect their wharf.

Mr John Hughes, piermaster, Menai Bridge, explained how the rafts were brought from the ships to the wharf and said that the extension of St. George's Pier would assist the firm in doing so and so would the removal of the Prince's Pier. '*At present, it was dangerous to land goods at the St. George's Pier (the stone pier) and if the piles and girder bridge on the Prince's Pier were removed, that would be a better place to land goods than the St. George's Pier,*' he said.

John Williams, boatman, also thought that the proposed extension of St. George's Pier would greatly help in the navigation of Messrs Roberts' rafts. It would have helped them very much the previous week, when a raft went against the Prince's Pier.

Mr RW Roberts said the firm of *William Roberts and Co.* were timber importers and general merchants. They also had a large sawmill business. During his recollection, the company rented the quay, and chartered ships to bring cargoes. They discharged their timber under Craig y Don, where they rafted it, and it took 12 or 14 days for a vessel to break bulk (discharge the timber).

Mr JR Davies declared he was the lessee of Prince's Pier and the adjoining wharf and had use of the foreshore since around 1837.

Although he did not oppose the pier he was concerned that the rafts might be swept by the tide into the dangerous Swellies.[8]

Agreement was reached and the Act was passed. The Council had bought up the foreshore around Prince's Pier in the 1890s and secured the freehold of St George's Pier (the old stone pier) together with its buildings and foreshore. Plans were then made for a new promenade and pier.

1903 the promenade nearing completion (top) & St Tudno II arriving shortly after opening 1904 (Menai Heritage)

---

[8] Carnarvon and Denbigh Herald & N & S Wales Independent 23 May 1902

The loading and unloading of the many cargoes of timber was done with the use of rafts, as the report from the new pier hearing shows. The large sailing ships anchored out in the Strait and the timber was unloaded on to rafts which were then floated in towards the Yard ready for lifting on to the quay.

There are stories of floating the timber on the tides, chained together as in North America and one instance of towing the timber to the growing resort of Llandudno and leaving it on the beach, as there were no landing facilities.

The *North Wales Chronicle* (31 July 1869) reports an accident in which **John Bagnall**, was seriously injured, whilst using the winch to off-load a cargo of Davies' timber near Craig y Don from the *Chanticleer* - a barque, built in North Shields by John R Kelso in 1862.

The Crane 2016

Other goods were regularly brought in by steamer for the people of Anglesey. Because of the state of the old stone pier all shipping had been using Prince's Pier.

Those vessels, which could moor alongside the quay on Prince's Pier, obviously made use of cranage. The crane on Prince's Pier is shown on the 1889 map and may even have been installed during the lease of the quay by the *City of Dublin Steam Packet Company* (1873- 1878). There is also mention of a crane on the end of the stone pier during the building of the new pier, 1904.

In 1891 the Quay was listed as Prince's Landing Stage and finally in 1901, the address is **Prince's Pier**, with John Hughes as **piermaster**. Jack (John) Roberts, age 69, is living on Cambria Road and listed as a mariner (seas).

T he New St. George's Pier created a whole new facility for Menai Bridge. David Lloyd George opened it on 10th September 1904 and was presented with a golden key.

THE CEREMONY. The party having been photographed by Mr J. Wickens, Bangor, a procession was formed of the members of the Council, Menai Bridge Boys' Brigade and Bugle Band, a detachment of the "Clio" boys*, and the Fire Brigade, who presented a very smart appearance. At the pier gates the "Clio" boys and the Boys' Brigade formed a guard of honour, and the Chairman read the following address of welcome to Mr Lloyd George: "We, the Menai Bridge District Council, desire to express our gratification that you should once again visit our little town ....

Being thus pre-eminently a people's pier, it is but fitting that in choosing the person to perform the crowning ceremony the Council should decide upon one who is so truly a representative of the "werin."**

The North Wales Express, 16th September 1904

*the locally sited training ship
**the people

It was a grand occasion and a proud moment of success for the Urban District Council.

The ease with which passengers could disembark resulted in greatly increased numbers of visitors to the town. This was the heyday of day trips and thousands of people disembarked from the paddle steamers at the new pier.

There was a promenade with room to stroll, meet people and chat. Entry

John Hughes at Pier gates (Syd Hughes)

charges were taken at the gatehouse. It was indeed 'a people's pier' as had been envisaged.

The Brass Band held concerts on Friday and Saturday evenings but was only allowed to use a collection box to raise funds. There were stalls and vending machines on the promenade but there was no trading allowed on Sundays.

Visitors on the promenade (Menai Heritage)

Menai Bridge Brass Band Concert programme 1915 (Menai Heritage)

The Urban District Council had been working tirelessly for a considerable time to develop the town as a tourist resort. As well as the promenade and pier, another requirement was a pavilion for concerts. Councillor J G Bacon loaned the money to build the pavilion.[9]

However, the *Liverpool and North Wales Steam Ship Co* (founded in 1890) were unhappy to find that numbers of visitors and thus income was declining. They announced the service to Menai Bridge would be cut.

[9] St George's Pier 1904 -2004 – Menai Bridge Civic Society

The Council were intent on developing tourism for the town and so were forced to negotiate with other companies to improve the numbers. There were various steamship companies at the time and their efforts were successful.

La Marguerite was brought into service on the North Wales route in 1904 – a big expensive ship she brought hundreds of visitors to Menai Bridge, able to disembark at the new pier.

La Marguerite 1904 (Menai Heritage)

Sadly, after a dutiful service John Hughes became ill and died in 1908 age 55 years.

In loving memory of
John Hughes
Pier Master, Menai Bridge
born August 31st 1854
died July 16th 1908
'Faithful unto death'
also of Margaret
the beloved wife of the above
born April 27th 1848
died March 15th 1935
'until he cometh at rest'

John Hughes grave, plot B016, St Tysilio

Menai Bridge OBITUARY. The death took place on Thursday, after a long illness, of Mr John Hughes, who for the last 35 years has been piermaster of Menai Bridge, under the Dublin Company, the Liverpool and North Wales Steamship Company, and the Menai Bridge District Council, who are the owners of the present pier. Deceased, who was 55 years of age, was very popular in the district, his genial and courteous manner earning for him the esteem of many. He leaves a widow and three sons and one daughter. One of the sons is out in Canada, and another is acting his father's deputy on the pier.

Carnarvon & Denbigh Herald, 24th July 1908

After the death of his father, **John Gray Hughes** took over the role of Piermaster, Harbourmaster, and Collector of Dues. He had been working as Deputy Piermaster for a while.

Prior to the opening of the new St George's Pier, Prince's Pier had been used by all shipping – tolls and dues amounting to £495 in 1903.

But with the opening of the new St George's Pier, the Piermaster was responsible for both piers. John Gray is listed in 1911 census as Piermaster for Menai Bridge Urban District Council.

He achieved a record during his lifetime, by being on the pontoon to meet every Liverpool steamer arriving at Menai Bridge.

A fter the death of his father, John and his mother continued to live in the Pierhouse. His uncle Owen emigrated to Murrayville, Canada in 1911.[10] His aunt

John Gray Hughes (1882- 1970) on the left, with Joe MacNamee, St Trillo (Menai Heritage)

---

[10] Syd Hughes

Catherine (Caddi) was a dressmaker and still at home whilst Uncle William appears to be working for the Post Office as a Sorting Clerk and Telegraphist and lodging in Whitchurch.

This was a busy time for the shipping – the steamers arrived daily, bringing goods and passengers. The sailing ships were still bringing timber from North America and there was coastal trade to Cardiff and London.

Menai Bridge town was thriving – visitors arrived in their hundreds for holidays as well as day trips. There were popular rail and steamer round trips, the local hotels and tea rooms were doing well, the public houses were numerous.

But that was all to change.

In August 1914 war was declared with Germany and many young men from Menai Bridge signed up to fight for their country. Tourism at its height was stopped overnight. *La Marguerite* having brought so many visitors to Menai Bridge was immediately requisitioned along with the crew. Because of her large capacity she was commissioned to be a troop carrier. The 6th Battalion City of London Regiment were the first troops to sail from Southampton to Le Havre during WW1. She covered over 52,000 miles during the war and carried some 360,000 troops to France.

The vessel did so many trips that she was worn out. At the end of the war she was handed back to her owners, remaining in service until 1925 but eventually being scrapped.

The men on the pier, sailors and seamen were needed for naval service.

Following school, John Gray Hughes had served on the steamships sailing from Liverpool to New York – *SS Hemisphere*, and then as AB on the *SS Quernmore* and *SS Rowanmore* (Johnston & Co). Aged 16, he signed on the *St Elvies* with the *Liverpool and North Wales Steam Ship Company*, and would have worked his way to Menai Bridge as a crew member.

The Menai Bridge Roll of Service is held in the Memorial Rooms on Water St and lists the soldiers and sailors with details of their regiments and ships of service. John Hughes is listed as serving on *La Marguerite* Trans(porter), the vessel which took so many soldiers across the Channel.

John Charles Jones was a local man, who had always lived near the Strait. Born in 1887, son of John and Mary Jones of the Cross Keys Inn, he was working as a baker in 1911 and spoke Welsh and English. He was secretary for the Menai Bridge Football team in 1913 and would have been aware that most of the team signed up straight away when war was declared. The newspapers reported that 57 men from Menai Bridge had signed up for the Army and the Navy in the first two months since war was declared.

John Charles Jones (Lynne & Mike O'Regan)

The Paulina (formerly The Queen Mother. (Lynne & Mike O'Regan)

Working on the pier he would have knowledge of the sea and shipping, and in 1916 he joined the Royal Navy and served on the armoured patrol yacht, *HM Paulina* with the Grand Fleet, 1917/1918. He was in the East until the cessation of hostilities.[11]

The Royal Naval Volunteer Reserves (later Royal Naval Reserves) were based in Menai Bridge, and administered mine clearance services. Motor Patrol boats were moored at Prince's Pier on Armistice Day 1918. On the Roll of Service there is listed **Robert Ellis** of the Royal Naval Reserves.

Nov 11th 1918 Armistice Day at Prince's Pier (Menai Heritage)

---

[11] North Wales Chronicle 1933

1918 and those who had survived the war returned to Menai Bridge. John Charles Jones returned to be assistant piermaster on the new St George's Pier until his death by accident in the 1930s. He did much charitable work for the town – for the men who returned from the war to face life with disabilities and no work.

A newspaper report shows that he was instrumental in the raising of the Menai Bridge War Memorial following the conflict; convening the initial meeting and raising money for the purpose. He also established the Memorial Rooms and the beginnings of the British Legion, taking on the role of Secretary.

John Charles Jones – assistant piermaster
(Lynne O Regan)

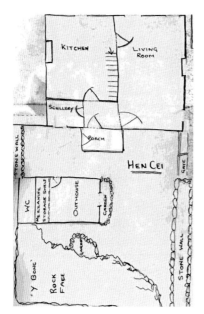

Plan of Pierhouse, drawn by Vivienne Burke

John G Hughes completed his active service too and returned to his role as piermaster until his retirement. He married Mary Cecilia Rice in 1919 and their son Dennis Gray was born in 1921.

The steamer trade was re-established after the war but never reached the same proportions as previously. Both piers were still used for goods. The timber wharf was used by *Isolde* in the 1930s.

Dennis grew up in the Pierhouse, no doubt learning the role of Piermaster from his father. Vivienne Burke, his stepdaughter, remembers visiting Dennis and her mother in the three-bedroomed house in later years.

The icy January winds howl around the house on Prince's Pier, but inside Mr. Hughes finds contentment and relaxation by the fireside.

John Gray Hughes, North Wales Chronicle, 1959 (Jennifer Jones)

The little garden at the back grew a few vegetables and flowers. She remembers the cosiness of the living kitchen where John Gray Hughes would warm himself by the fire after a cold spell on the pier.

In the 1930s, relatives of Dennis built a house on Y Bonc (the rock behind the Pierhouse). It was a beautiful 1930s Art Deco design, shown in the Ideal Home magazine - maintaining the tradition of the site as a place of innovation.

The house on Y Bonc built 1933 (Fiona Rowlands)

St George's Pier continued to be 'the people's pier' with concerts, dancing and events in the pavilion.

Concert on the pier – 1930s (Menai Heritage)

But Prince's Pier was a working site. In the 1920s the warehouse had been let to John Blyth of Liverpool, for use as a distribution centre. Deliveries made to the quay, would have required the services of the Piermaster to deal with the goods and provide the vessels with water and fuel.

During WWII both piers came under the control of the Admiralty. A large shed was built in front of the warehouse on the Quay, where it remained until the 1960s.

There were Nissan huts at the top of the Porth y Wrach slipway (one to be used later by Donald Smith)

Prince's Pier warehouse & shed
(Fiona Rowlands)

The next generation of the Hughes family were called up to serve their country and in 1943 the sons of Owen Hughes in Canada – Gwilym and John – visited their relatives on the Pier.

The War Department continued to occupy the Prince's Pier until 1959. After the derequisitioning of the pier, various alternative uses were considered but none with great success.

After the war the Hughes family were living in Pier House in the 1950s but the Quay was not accessible to local people. It was still a working site.

Donald Smith, a 2nd Lieutenant in the Royal Electrical and Mechanical Engineers was posted to Menai Bridge for a year in 1953. The Maritime Unit of the Royal Army Service Corps 45 Company, had been based at Prince's Pier, from 1939 and would remain until 1960.

1943 turnstile to St George's Pier. Gwilym Owen Hughes (1921-2007) and John Gray Hughes (1915-1977) with their uncle, piermaster John Gray Hughes (1882-1970)
(Syd Hughes)

He writes:

This Unit operated a small fleet of boats. These were 50- foot Dickens Class General Service Vessels which had been built between 1943 and 1947 and were named after Dickens characters. Additionally, there were Battles Class High Speed Target Towing Launches which had been complete between 1944 and 1945.

The role was to provide an air sea rescue service to RAF Valley and to tow targets which were used by the Royal Artillery Coastal Defence Batteries located at appropriate places along the coast of the UK at that time.

I was in charge of a small workshop staffed by around twenty civilians employed by the army.

Office nameplate (Donald Smith)

During the late 1950s the Royal Army Service Corps vessels from Menai Bridge played a large part in rescuing people, equipment and documents from the training vessel **Conway** which was moored in the Menai Straits and had caught fire.

HMS Conway – training ship (Menai Heritage)

Jocelyn and Mike Bowen remember Prince's Pier being a prohibited area with big KEEP OUT signs. In the 1940s a loaded truck had driven off the pier and into the Strait, shedding its load of ammunition. It was winched back up at low tide but searching for interesting contraband remained a favourite activity of the local children for many years.

Inside the pier pavilion (Jocelyn & Mike Bowen)

St George's Pier remained a favourite with the people of Menai Bridge. The Pavilion was well used for concerts, dances films and meetings. Slot machines were placed on the Promenade for entertainment. The 'people's pier' was a place of fun after the miseries of war.

Daily life in Menai Bridge continued.

The commandeering of Prince's Pier was terminated in 1959 allowing both piers to resume continuous use. There was always plenty to do. Goods arrived and had to be unloaded. Vessels took on water and fuel and moored overnight.

Rowland and Wil Williams of Rallt farm, on their milk round outside the Woodyard buildings, Porth Daniel (Menai Heritage)

St Tudno first voyage of the season 1960
(Vivienne Burke)

The growing popularity of motor cars and buses was affecting the business of the *Liverpool and North Wales Steam Ship Co*. Numbers of passengers were falling but there was still a daily service to Menai Bridge. In this commemorative photograph, John Gray Hughes welcomes the *St Tudno* for the first visit of the season in 1960, with members of the Urban District Council and the steamship company.

Dennis took over as Piermaster from his father, on his retirement in 1961 and work continued.

A glimpse into the future and Dennis would see that he is to marry, in 1967, to Lucia Kelly (nee Staczkiewcz) and experience life as part of a large gregarious Polish family living in the Liverpool area, so very different from his previous quiet years. And that in 1983 when he dies, the Hughes family on the Pier will come to an end – three generations of

Piermasters covering more than a century; thousands of visitors; tons of timber; hundreds of emigrants leaving for another world; births, marriages and deaths and many fond memories of times on the pier. The end of an era for the Pier House.

Bunkering' fuel on Prince's Pier in 1964 when St George's Pier was being altered. Left to right H Humphries, mate, HW Walker and DG Hughes. (Menai Heritage)

B ack to reality – as darkness began to fall over the Strait, Dennis drifted back to reality – to the day to day work on the Piers. With a last look at all its magnificence, he turned away to lock up the gates and take his memories home. Time for a warm by the fire in *Hen Cei* and a word with his father about the day to come. Tomorrow would bring the *St Tudno* again and no doubt the children would still be up to their tricks!

St Tudno arriving at St George's Pier (Menai Heritage)

Dennis Hughes at gates of the pier (Syd Hughes)

Credits

With sincere thanks to everyone who has helped in this community production:

Menai Heritage Collection Panel (Rodger and Alun for sourcing and scanning Archive material).

John Cowell for items from his collection as well as active assistance with content.

Family archive material:

Phyl Barlow (James Black)
Jocelyn and Mike Bowen
Vivienne Burke (Hughes family)
Geraint Edwards (Edwards grocers)
Syd Hughes (Hughes family)
Jennifer Jones (Hughes family)
Claudia Moore (Alonzo Greaves)
Lynne O'Regan (John Charles Jones)
Fiona Rowlands (Y Bonc)
Donald Smith (Wartime base)

References:

David Longley – *Prince's Pier*, Gwynedd Archaeological Trust Project no 1873
John Cowell – *Menai Bridge – A Pictorial History*
Aled Eames – *Ships and Seamen of Anglesey and Ventures in Sail*
Gwynedd Family History Society - Memorial Inscriptions of the Church of St Tysilio
Robert Cadwalader, Criccieth – maritime expertise

Julie Stone – Menai Heritage volunteer – text and community liaison

Warren Kovach - Menai Heritage volunteer – page design and layout and image processing

Location Map for the Piers

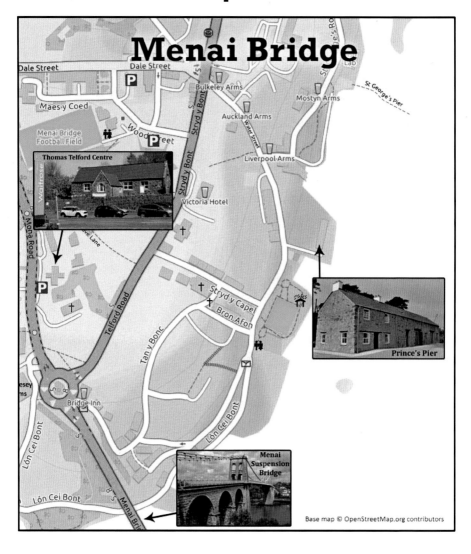